K-1
NUMBER SKILLS

DESIGNED TO REINFORCE ESSENTIAL MATH SKILLS!

By completing this math workbook your child will gain systematic practice in the following math concepts:

- Printing numbers 1-10
- Reading numbers 1-10
- Counting numbers 1-10
- More, less and the same
- Addition facts to 10
- Subtraction facts to 10

PRINTING NUMBERS 1 TO 5

1 1 1 1 1

2 2 2 2 2

3 3 3 3 3

4 4 4 4 4

5 5 5 5 5

PRINTING NUMBERS 6 TO 10

PRINTING
NUMBERS AND WORDS FROM 1-5

1	one	
2	two	
3	three	
4	four	
5	five	

PRINTING
NUMBERS AND WORDS FROM 6-10

6	six	
7	seven	
8	eight	
9	nine	
10	ten	

COUNTING 1-5

Count the number of things in each row.
Circle the correct numeral.

1 2 3 4 5

1 2 3 4 5

1 2 3 4 5

1 2 3 4 5

1 2 3 4 5

1 2 3 4 5

NUMBERS 1-5

Use the colour key to colour the picture.

1	-	red
2	-	yellow
3	-	blue
4	-	brown
5	-	green

COUNT AND WRITE

How many?

Count and write the numbers.

COUNT AND WRITE

How many?

Count and write the numbers.

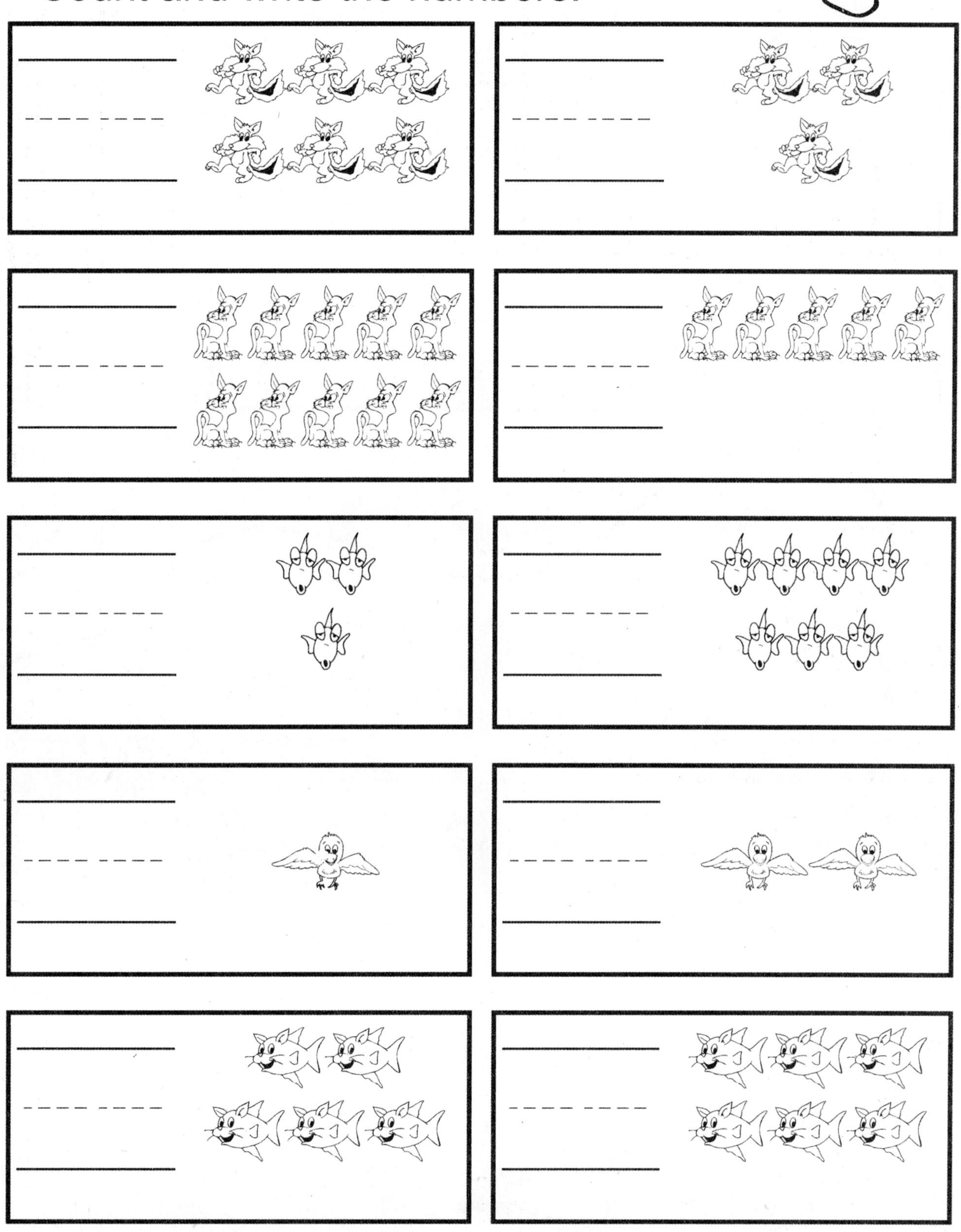

COUNT AND WRITE

Look at the picture.

How many of each sea creature?

DRAW THE NUMBER

Draw ○ to match each numeral.

three 3	six 6
nine 9	seven 7
eight 8	two 2
five 5	four 4

MORE OR LESS

Circle the set that has **less.**

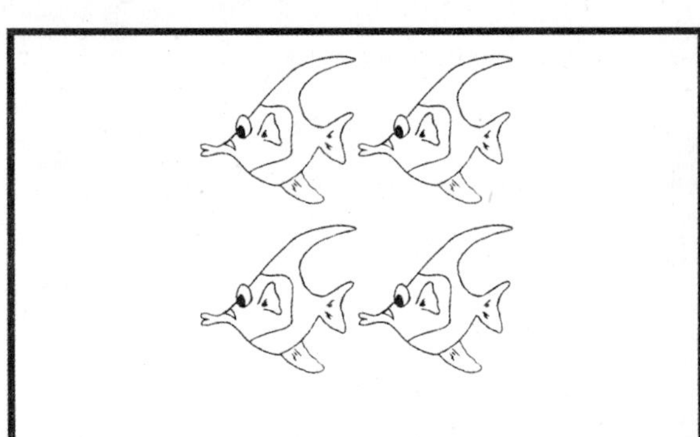

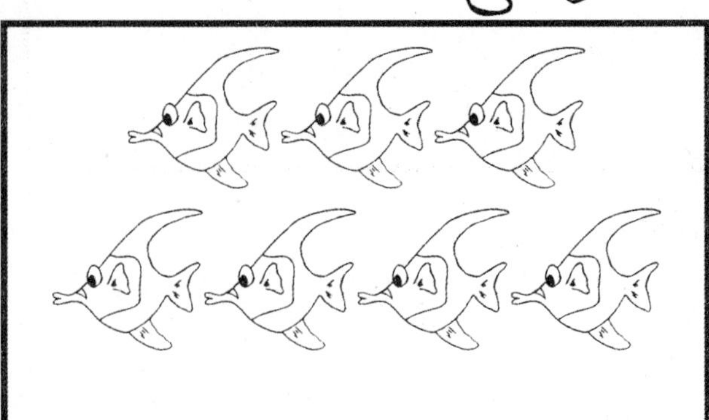

Circle the set that has **more.**

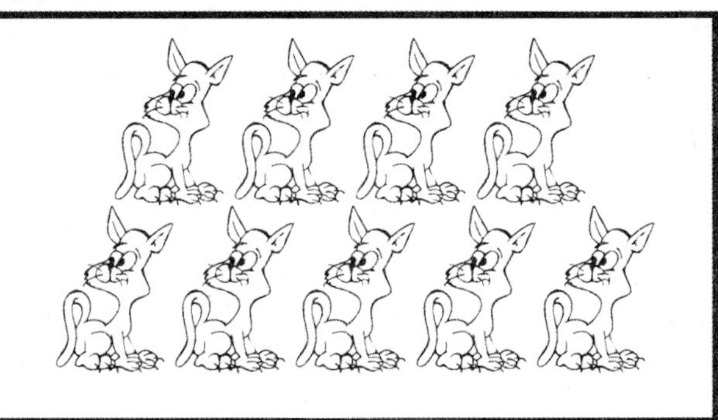

Circle the set that has **less.**

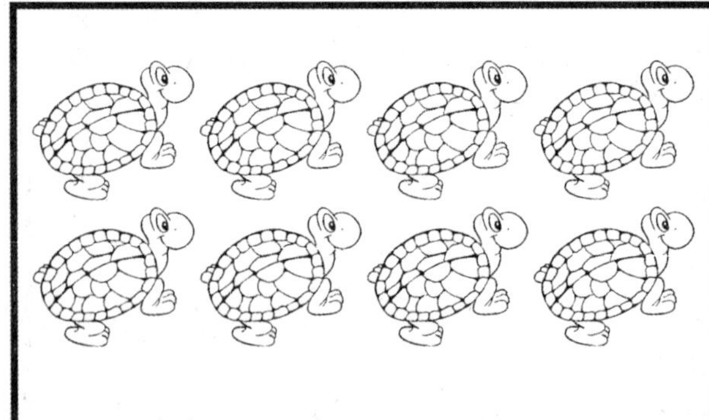

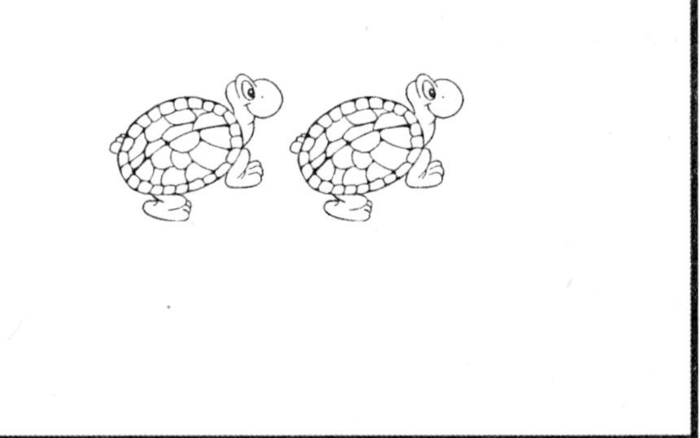

Circle the set that has **more.**

MORE, LESS, AND THE SAME

Look at the pictures.

Draw the pictures to make **more**, **less** or the **same**.

The first one is done for you.

 3	 more	 less	 same
 4	more	less	same
 5	more	less	same
 8	more	less	same

ADDITION FUN

Add the things together.
Write the number sentence.

_____ + _____ = _____

ADDITION FUN

Add the things together.
Write the number sentence.

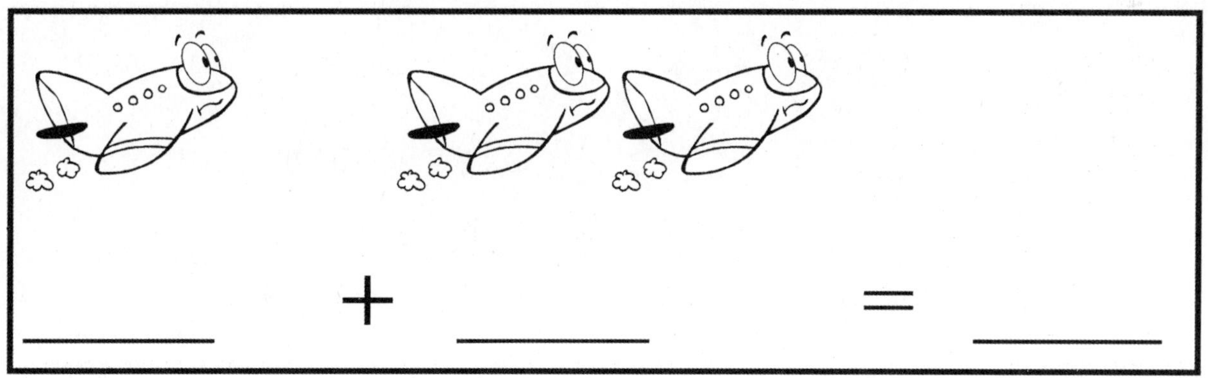

______ + ______ = ______

ADDITION FUN

Add the things together.
Write the number sentence.

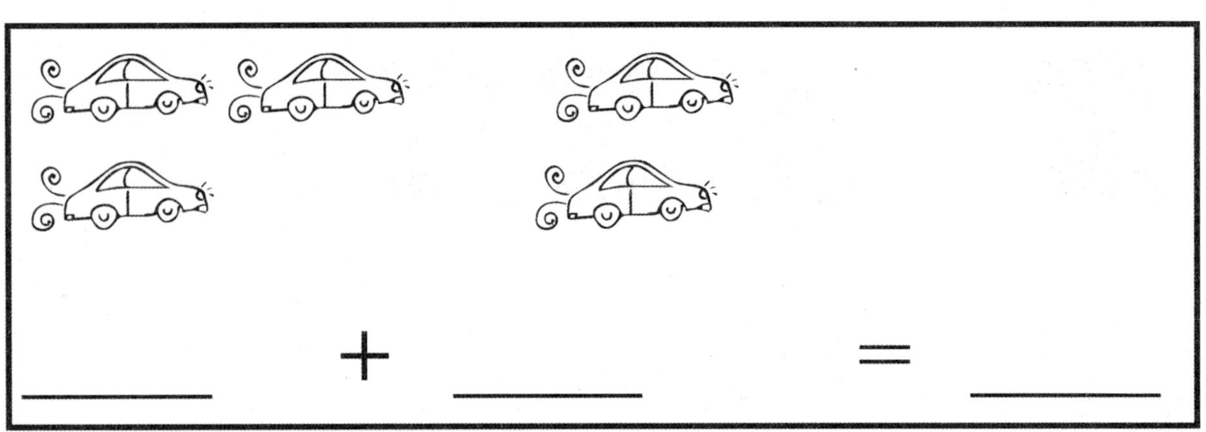

ADDITION FUN

Add the things together.
Write the number sentence.

______ + ______ = ______

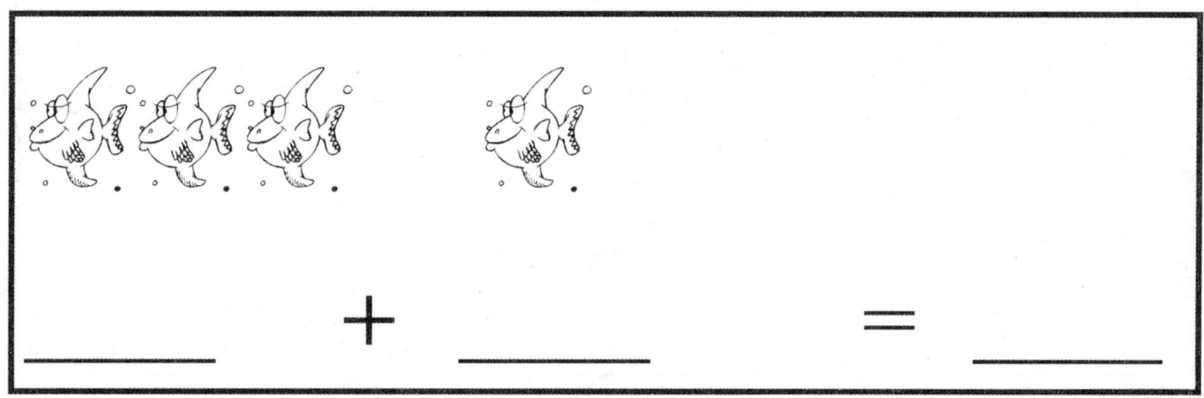

______ + ______ = ______

______ + ______ = ______

______ + ______ = ______

ADDITION FUN

Add the things together.
Write the number sentence.

______ + ______ = ______

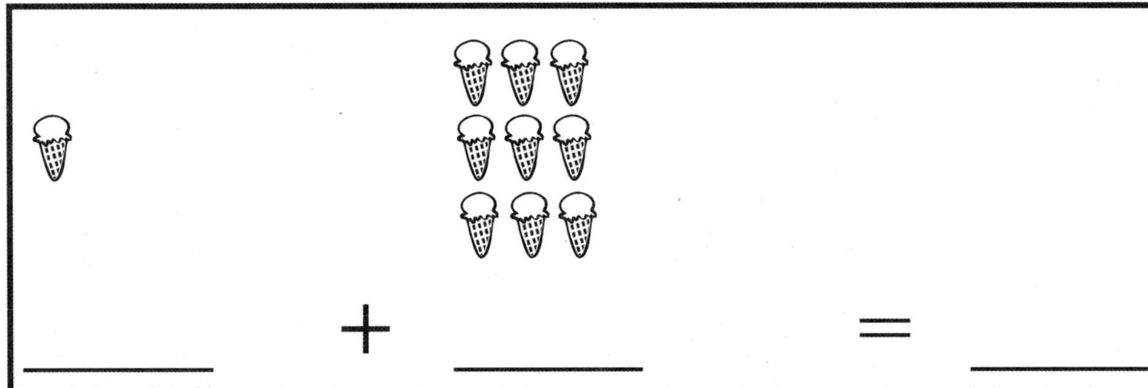

______ + ______ = ______

______ + ______ = ______

______ + ______ = ______

ADDITION FUN

Add the things together.
Write the number sentence.

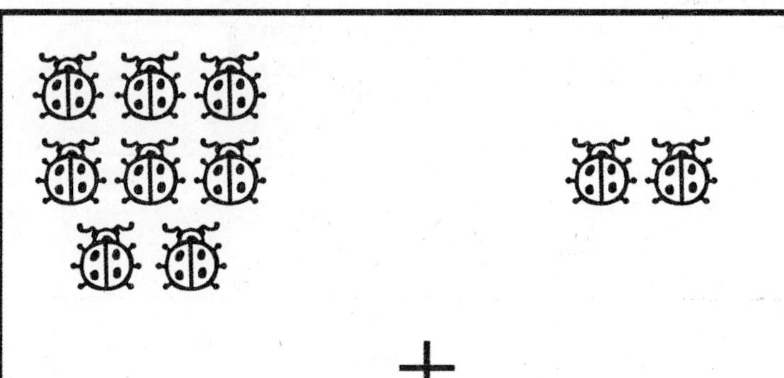

______ + ______ = ______

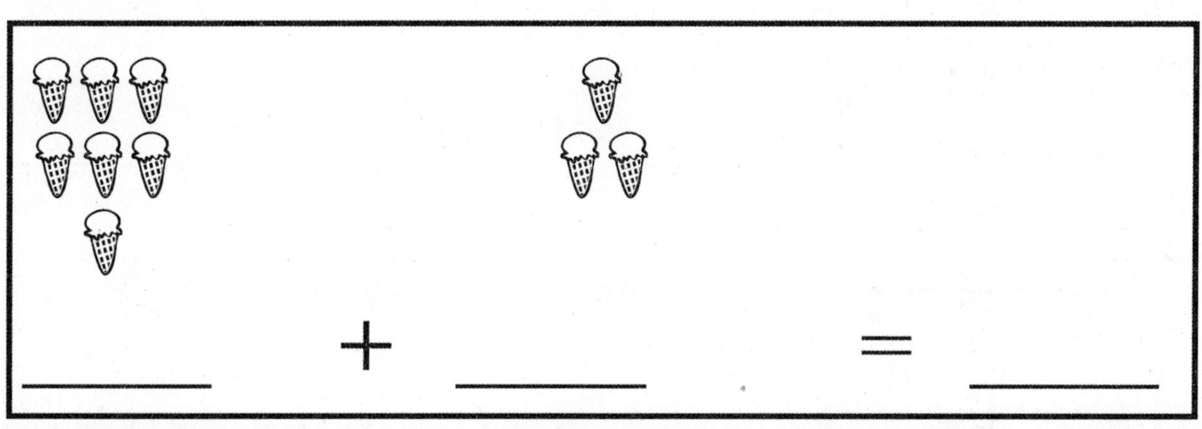

______ + ______ = ______

______ + ______ = ______

______ + ______ = ______

MORE ADDITION FUN

Add and write the sums.

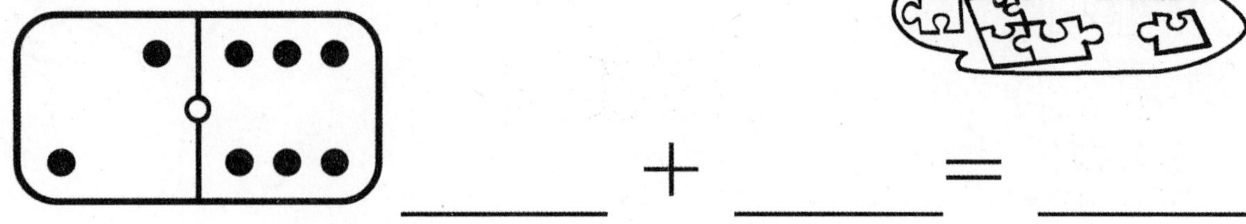

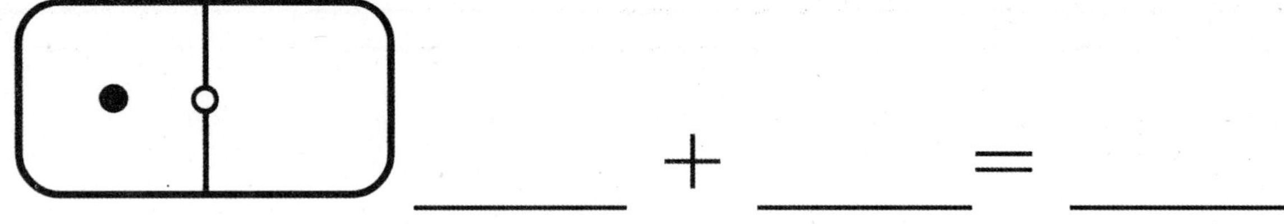

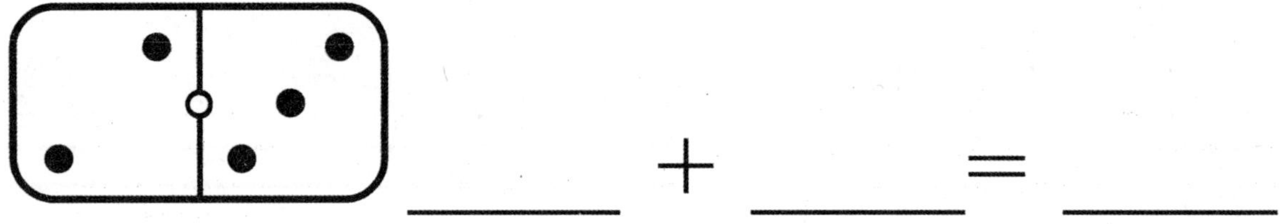

_____ + _____ = _____

_____ + _____ = _____

ADDITION DOUBLES

Add and write the sums.

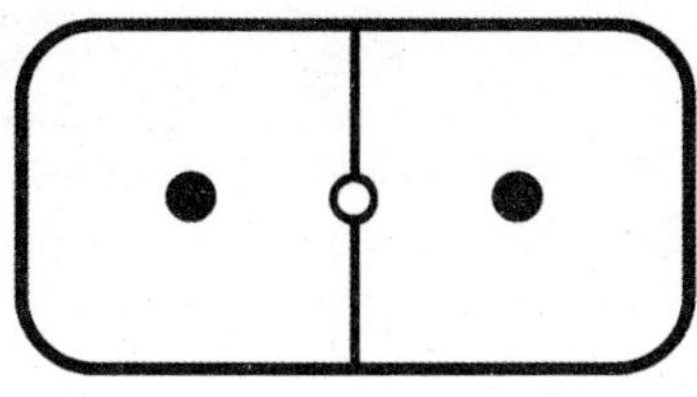

_____ + _____ = _____

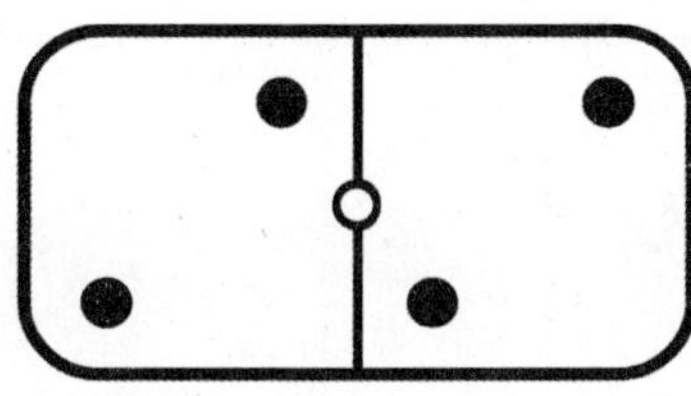

_____ + _____ = _____

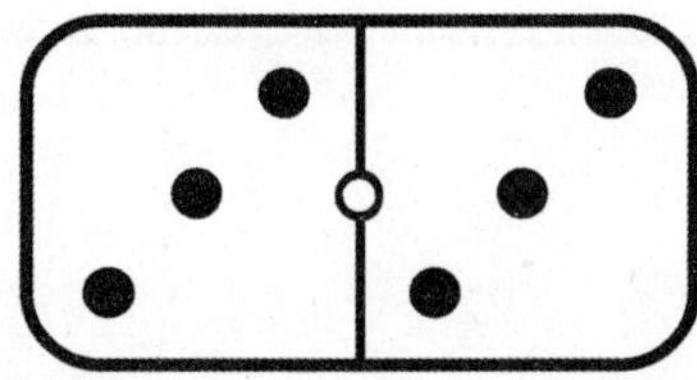

_____ + _____ = _____

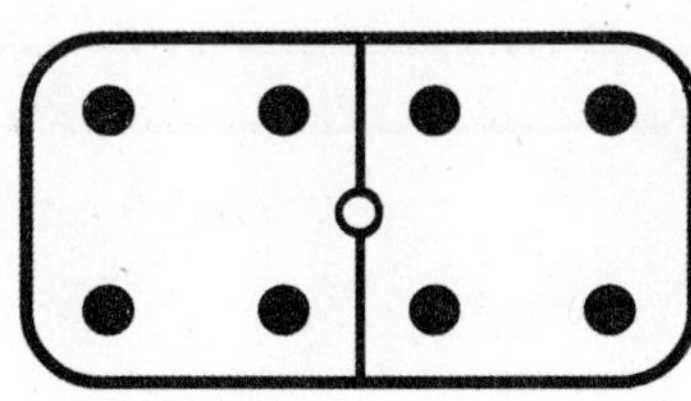

_____ + _____ = _____

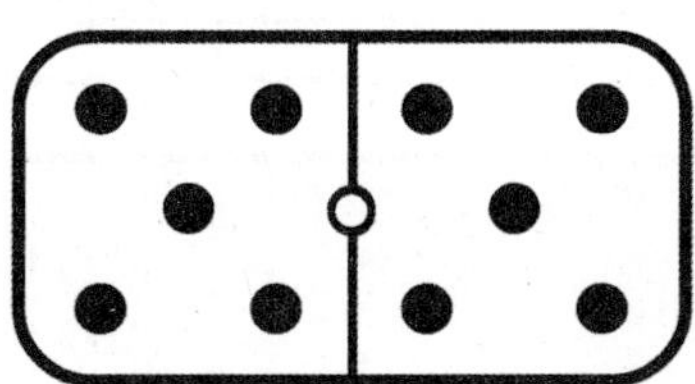

_____ + _____ = _____

SUBTRACTION FUN

Count the things and then take away.
Write the number sentence.

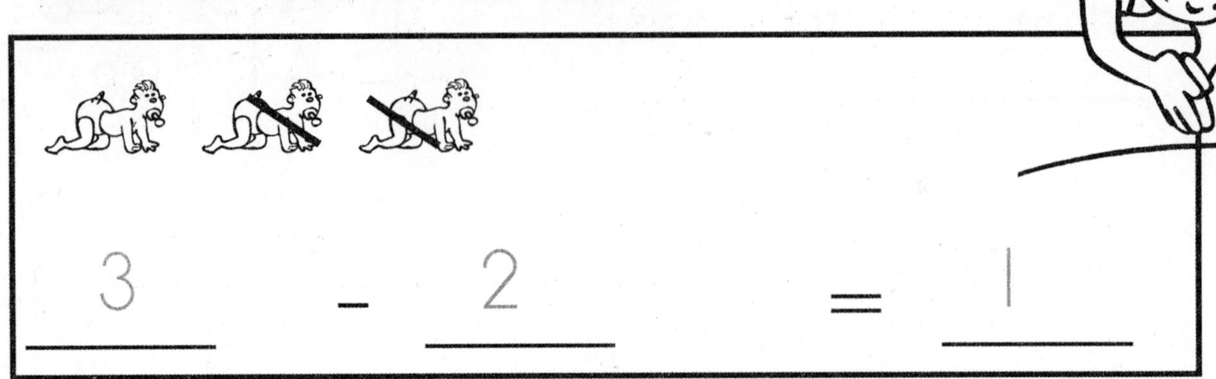

3 – 2 = 1

____ – ____ = ____

____ – ____ = ____

____ – ____ = ____

____ – ____ = ____

SUBTRACTION FUN

Count the things and then take away.
Write the number sentence.

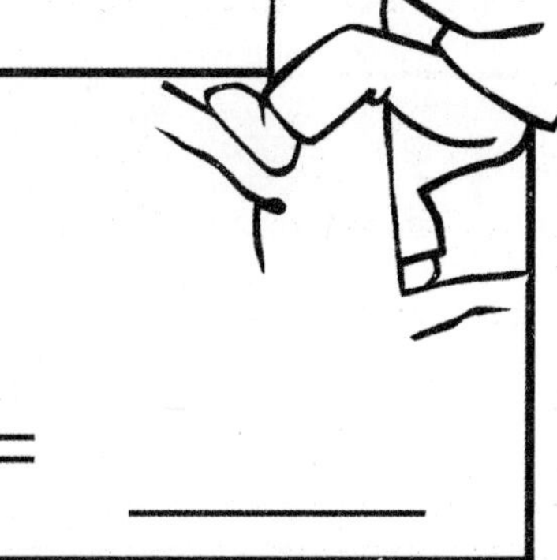

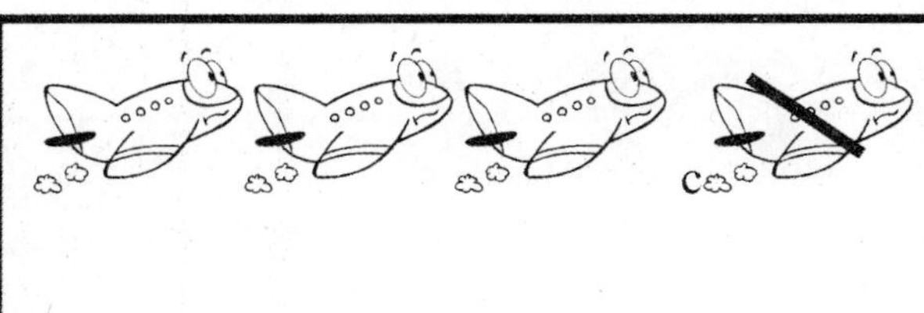

_______ – _______ = _______

_______ – _______ = _______

_______ – _______ = _______

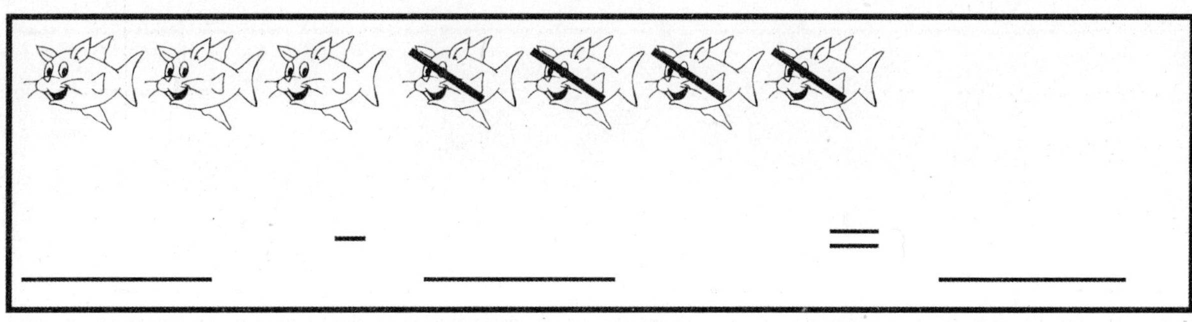

_______ – _______ = _______

_______ – _______ = _______

SUBTRACTION FUN

Count the things and take away.
Write the number sentence.

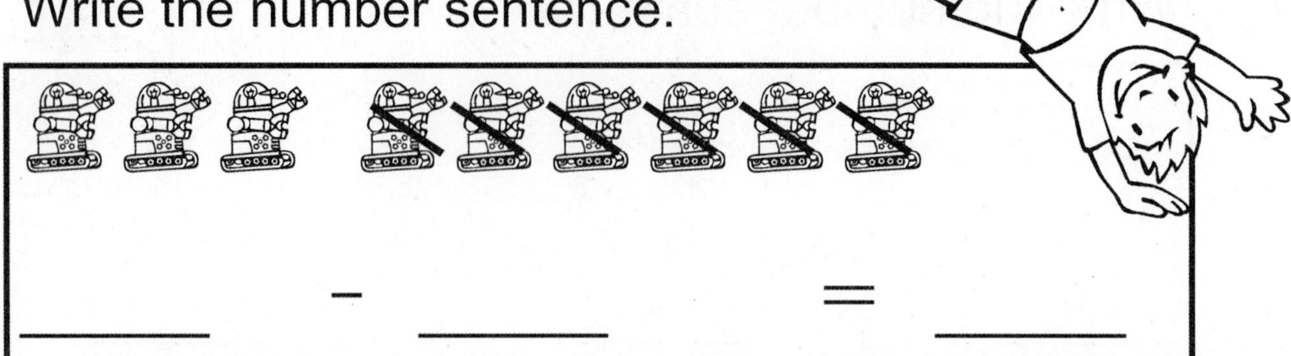

_______ – _______ = _______

_______ – _______ = _______

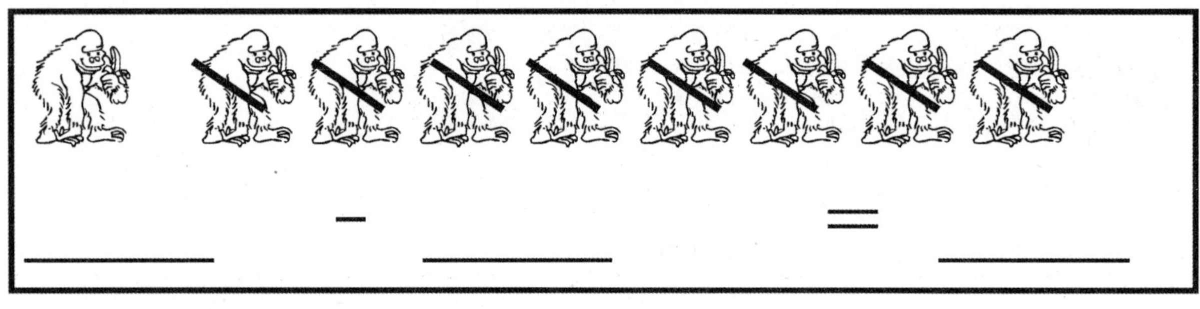

_______ – _______ = _______

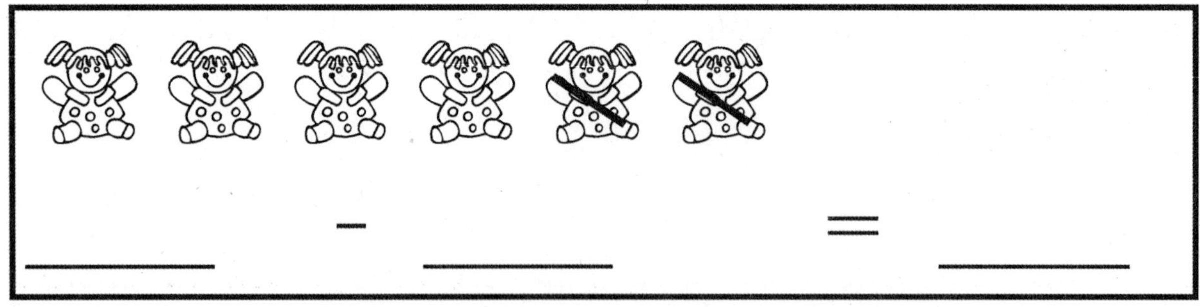

_______ – _______ = _______

_______ – _______ = _______

SUBTRACTION FUN

Count the things and take away.
Write the number sentence.

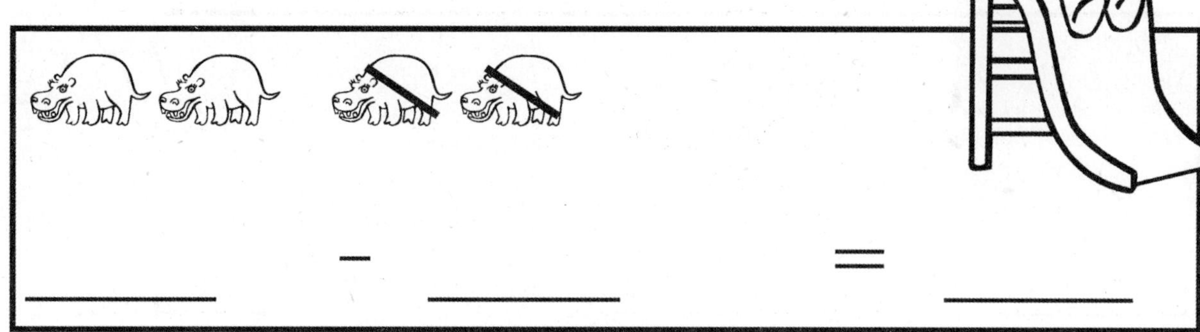

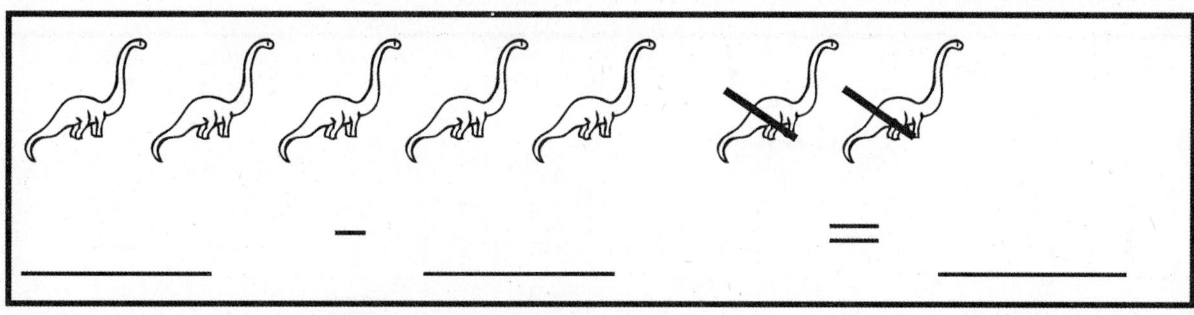

SUBTRACTION FUN

Count the things and take away.
Write the number sentence.

_______ – _______ = _______

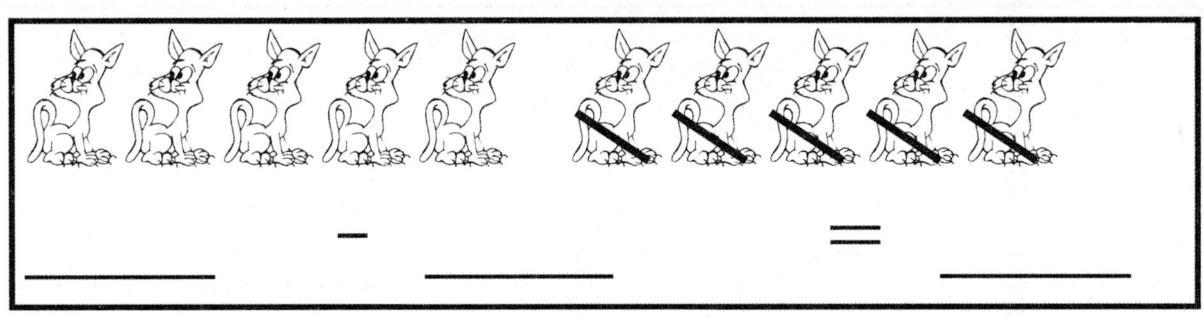

_______ – _______ = _______

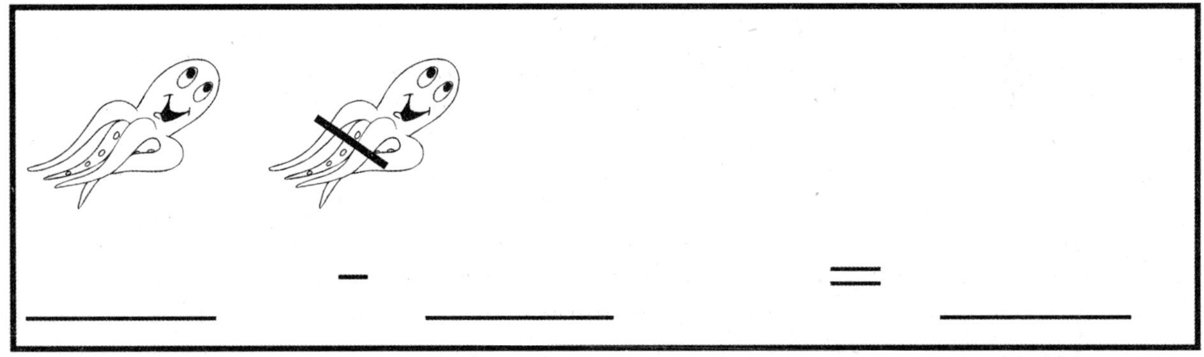

_______ – _______ = _______

_______ – _______ = _______

_______ – _______ = _______

SUBTRACTION FUN

Count the things and take away.
Write the number sentence.

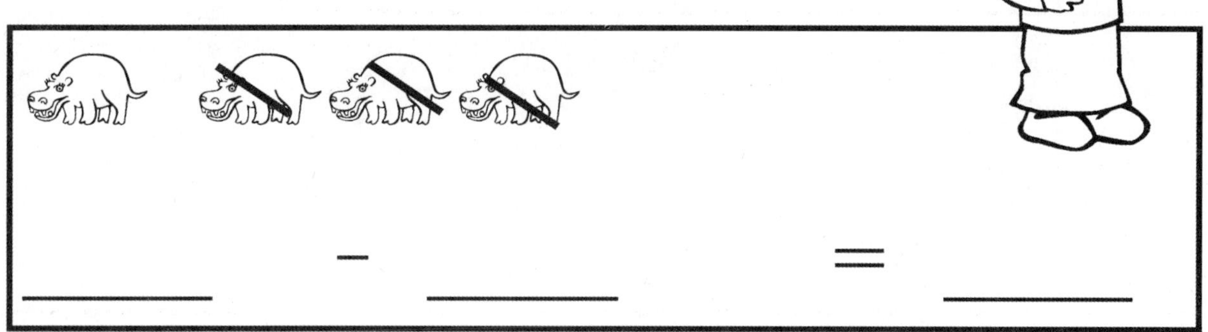

______ – ______ = ______

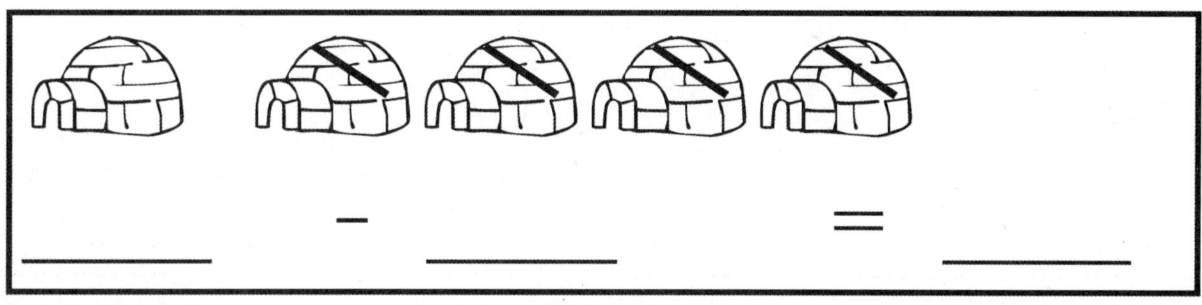

______ – ______ = ______

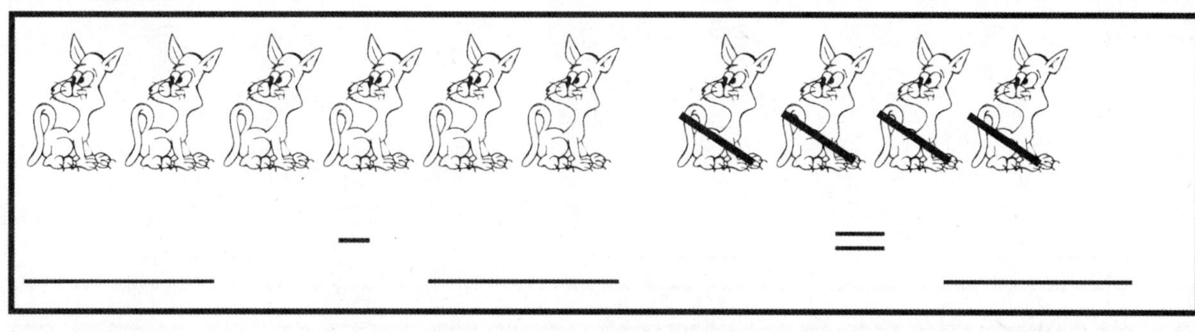

______ – ______ = ______

______ – ______ = ______

______ – ______ = ______

SUBTRACTION FUN

Count the things and take away.
Write the number sentence.

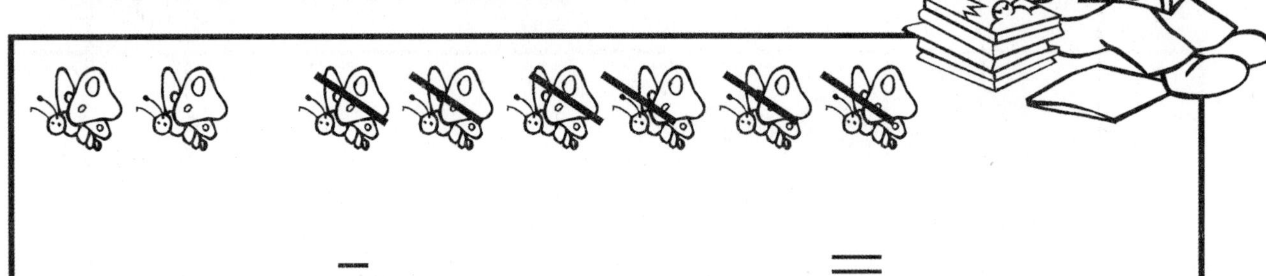

_______ − _______ = _______

_______ − _______ = _______

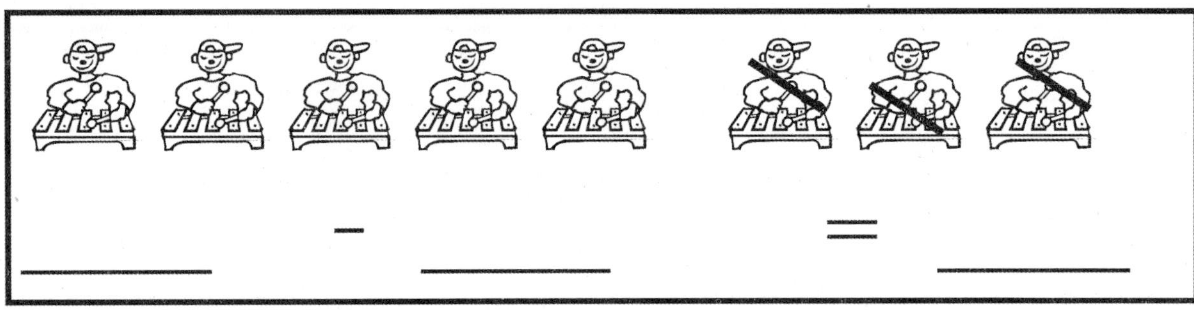

_______ − _______ = _______

_______ − _______ = _______

_______ − _______ = _______

ADDITION FACTS: SUMS TO 5

Complete the following sums
Use the number line to help.

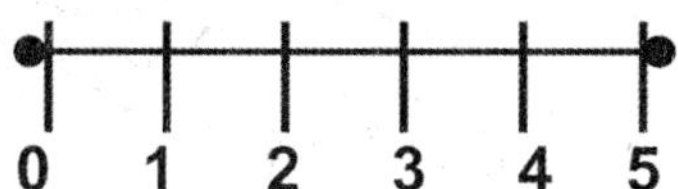

4+1= ___	3+1= ___	1+1= ___
2+0= ___	5+0= ___	2+3 = ___
1+3= ___	0+1= ___	0+5= ___
2+2= ___	1+4= ___	2+1= ___
1+0= ___	3+2= ___	4+0= ___
1+1= ___	0+0= ___	0+2= ___

ADDITION FACTS: SUMS TO 5

Complete the following sums
Use the number line to help.

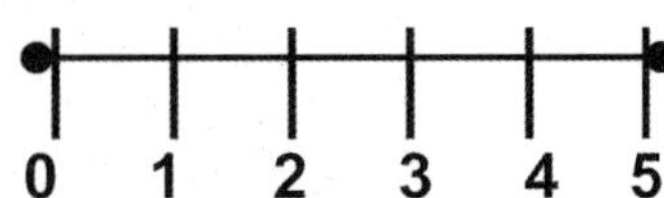

4 +1	2 +2	0 +2	1 +3
5 +0	1 +1	1 +2	3 +2
3 +1	4 +0	1 +4	2 +3
0 +1	2 +1	3 +1	1 +0

ADDITION FACTS: SUMS TO 7

Complete the following sums
Use the number line to help.

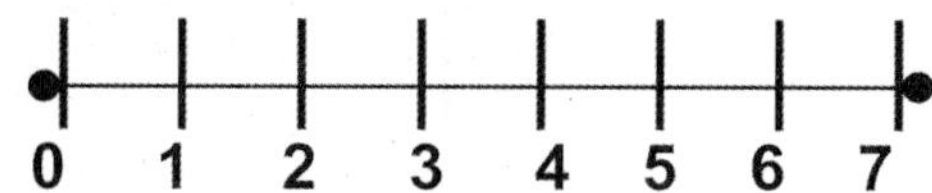

2+1= ___	1+1= ___	1+6= ___
5+2= ___	6+0= ___	0+3 =___
1+2= ___	4+3= ___	3+3= ___
2+2= ___	1+5= ___	2+4= ___
3+1= ___	2+3= ___	4+3= ___
2+5= ___	6+1= ___	3+3= ___

ADDITION FACTS: SUMS TO 7

Complete the following sums
Use the number line to help.

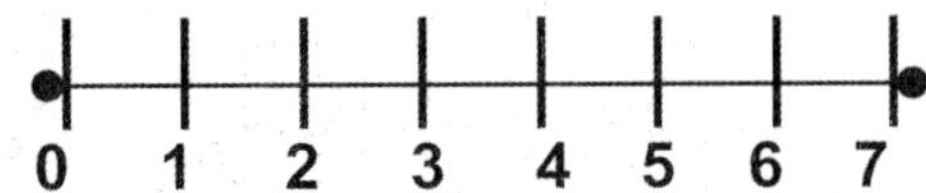

3 +1	1 +1	5 +2	3 +3
5 +0	2 +3	1 +2	3 +4
4 +3	4 +2	1 +3	2 +5
6 +1	4 +1	2 +2	1 +2

ADDITION FACTS: SUMS TO 10

Complete the following sums
Use the number line to help.

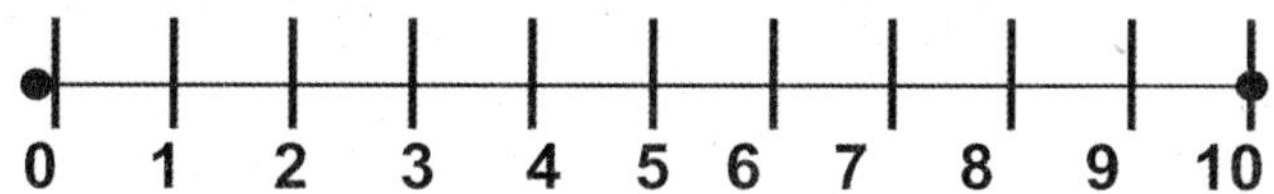

5+5= ___	2+6= ___	7+2= ___
2+2= ___	6+1= ___	3+3 = ___
4+4= ___	4+3= ___	2+3= ___
2+5= ___	1+5= ___	4+5= ___
1+1= ___	5+4= ___	4+3= ___
2+8= ___	6+1= ___	3+1= ___

ADDITION FACTS: SUMS TO 10

Complete the following sums
Use the number line to help.

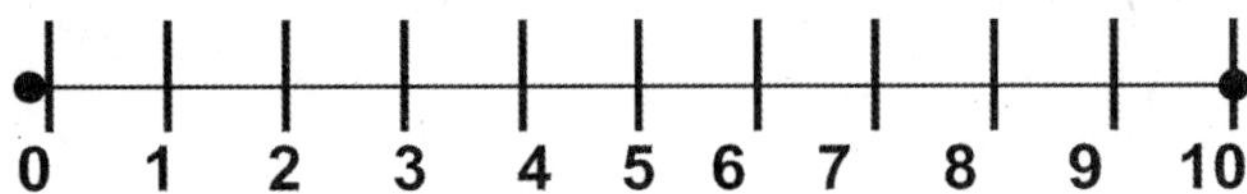

7 +2	5 +1	5 +2	8 +2
5 +3	2 +3	1 +4	6 +4
1 +3	4 +2	9 +1	2 +2
6 +2	2 +1	5 +5	3 +2

SUBTRACTION FACTS:
SUBTRACTING FROM 0 TO 5

Complete the following.
Use the number line to help.

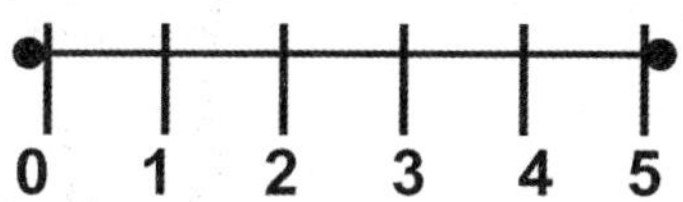

4-3= __	3-1= ___	5-4= ___
2-1= ___	2-0= __	3-3 = ___
3-2= ___	1-1= ___	4-0= ___
5-1= ___	1-0= ___	4-4= ___
4-2= ___	2-1= ___	4-1= ___
5-2= ___	5-5= ___	3-2= ___

SUBTRACTION FACTS:
SUBTRACTING FROM 0 TO 5

Complete the following.
Use the number line to help.

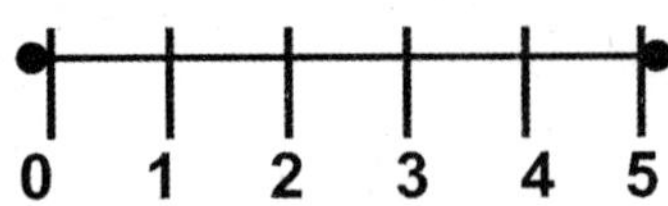

3 −1	5 −2	2 −2	3 −2
5 −0	1 −1	2 −0	3 −1
5 −4	4 −0	4 −2	2 −1
4 −3	2 −1	3 −1	1 −0

SUBTRACTION FACTS: SUBTRACTING FROM 0 TO 7

Complete the following.
Use the number line to help.

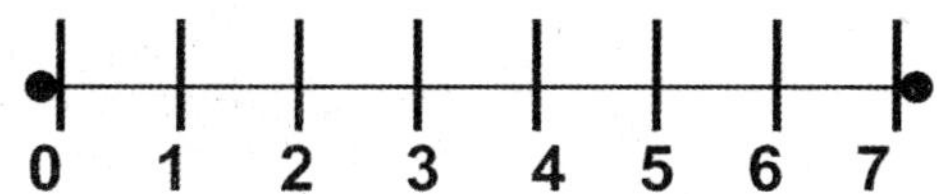

5−2= __	1−1= ___	6−4= ___
7−4= ___	6−2= __	7−3 =___
3−2= ___	4−3= ___	6−3= ___
2−1= ___	7−5= ___	2−0= ___
7−1= ___	4−2= ___	5−3= ___
6−5= ___	6−1= ___	7−6= ___

SUBTRACTION FACTS: SUBTRACTING FROM 0 TO 7

Complete the following.
Use the number line to help.

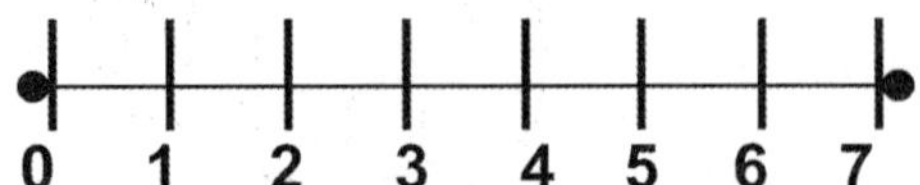

6 −3	3 −1	5 −1	7 −3
6 −2	3 −3	7 −4	3 −2
7 −5	4 −2	5 −3	6 −5
6 −1	4 −2	6 −2	7 −2

SUBTRACTION FACTS: SUBTRACTING FROM 1 TO 10

Complete the following sums
Use the number line to help.

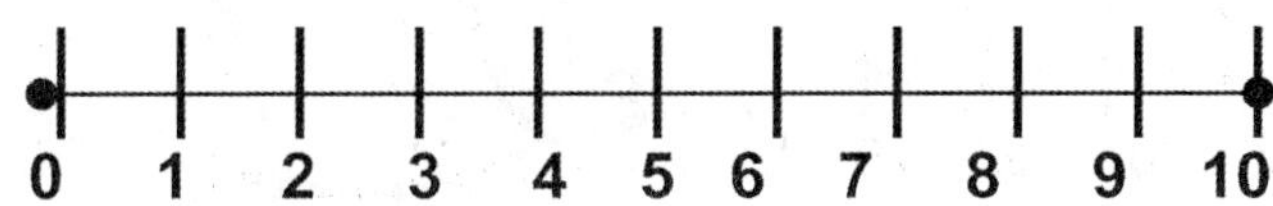

10-6= __	9-6= ___	1-0= ___
4-2= ___	6-1= __	8-3 =___
10-7= ___	4-3= ___	6-3= ___
10-8= ___	9-5= ___	3-1= ___
10-5= ___	5-4= ___	8-4= ___
7-4= ___	6-1= ___	10-3= ___

SUBTRACTION FACTS: SUBTRACTING FROM 1 TO 10

Complete the following sums
Use the number line to help.

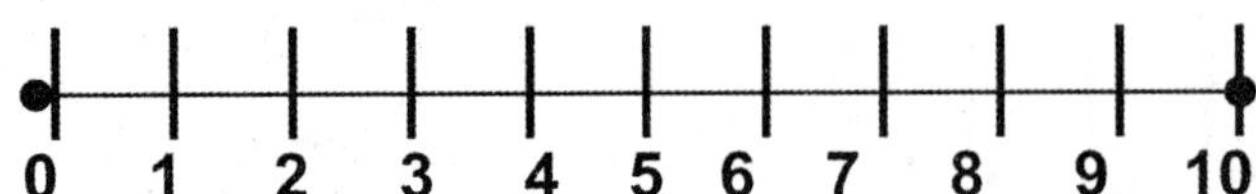

9 −2	1 −0	5 −2	10 −4
4 −3	5 −3	7 −6	8 −6
10 −7	10 −2	9 −1	9 −5
6 −2	8 −1	7 −5	3 −2

ADDITION FACTS: SUMS TO 5

Complete the following sums
Use the number line to help.

4+1= 5	3+1= 4	1+1= 2
2+0= 2	5+0= 5	2+3 = 5
1+3= 4	0+1= 1	0+5= 5
2+2= 4	1+4= 5	2+1= 3
1+0= 1	3+2= 5	4+0= 4
1+1= 2	0+0= 0	0+2= 2

ADDITION FACTS: SUMS TO 5

Complete the following sums
Use the number line to help.

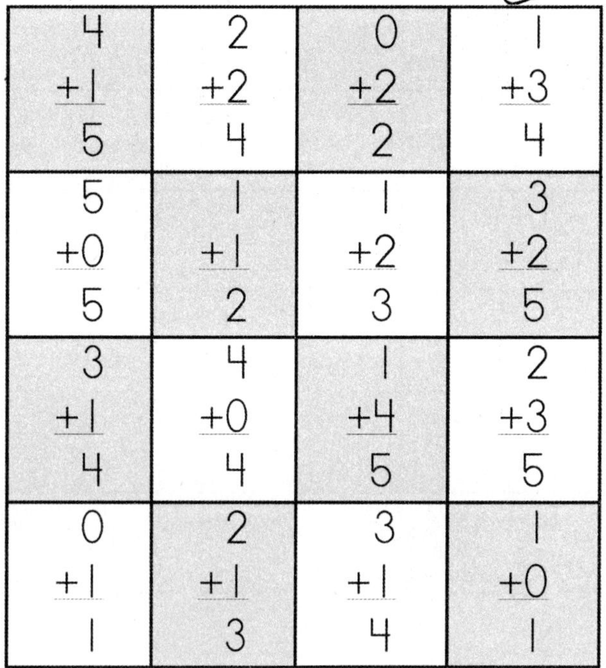

4 +1 5	2 +2 4	0 +2 2	1 +3 4
5 +0 5	1 +1 2	1 +2 3	3 +2 5
3 +1 4	4 +0 4	1 +4 5	2 +3 5
0 +1 1	2 +1 3	3 +1 4	1 +0 1

ADDITION FACTS: SUMS TO 7

Complete the following sums
Use the number line to help.

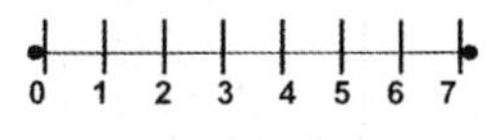

2+1= 3	1+1= 2	1+6= 7
5+2= 7	6+0= 6	0+3 = 3
1+2= 3	4+3= 7	3+3= 6
2+2= 4	1+5= 6	2+4= 6
3+1= 4	2+3= 5	4+3= 7
2+5= 7	6+1= 7	3+3= 6

ADDITION FACTS: SUMS TO 7

Complete the following sums
Use the number line to help.

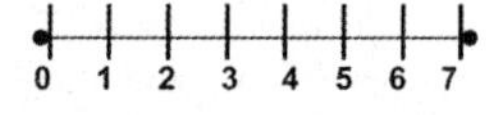

3 +1 4	1 +1 2	5 +2 7	3 +3 6
5 +0 5	2 +3 5	1 +2 3	3 +4 7
4 +3 7	4 +2 6	1 +3 4	2 +5 7
6 +1 7	4 +1 5	2 +2 4	1 +2 3

ADDITION FACTS: SUMS TO 10

Complete the following sums
Use the number line to help.

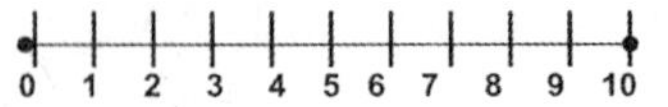

5+5= 10	2+6= 8	7+2= 9
2+2= 4	6+1= 7	3+3 = 6
4+4= 8	4+3= 7	2+3= 5
2+5= 7	1+5= 6	4+5= 9
1+1= 2	5+4= 9	4+3= 7
2+8= 10	6+1= 7	3+1= 4

ADDITION FACTS: SUMS TO 10

Complete the following sums
Use the number line to help.

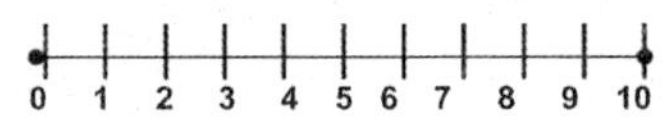

7 +2 9	5 +1 6	5 +2 7	8 +2 10
5 +3 8	2 +3 5	1 +4 5	6 +4 10
1 +3 4	4 +2 6	9 +1 10	2 +2 4
6 +2 8	2 +1 3	5 +5 10	3 +2 5

SUBTRACTION FACTS: SUBTRACTING FROM 0 TO 5

Complete the following.
Use the number line to help.

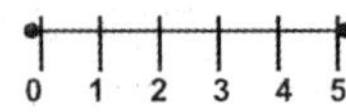

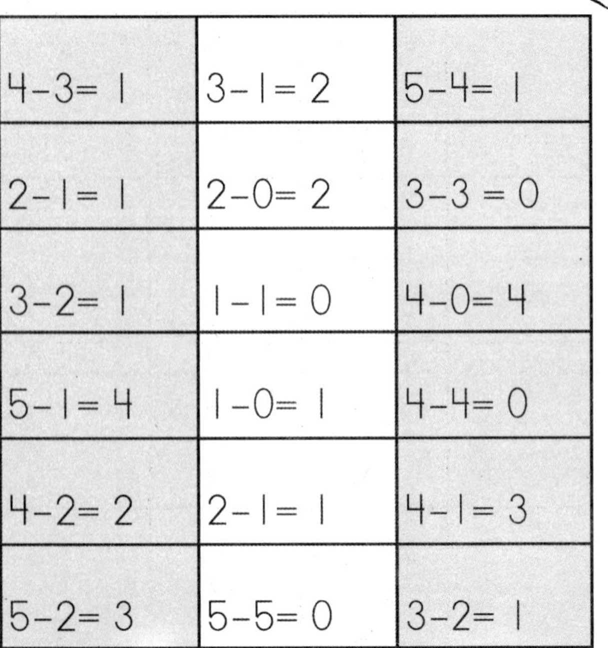

4-3= 1	3-1= 2	5-4= 1
2-1= 1	2-0= 2	3-3 = 0
3-2= 1	1-1= 0	4-0= 4
5-1= 4	1-0= 1	4-4= 0
4-2= 2	2-1= 1	4-1= 3
5-2= 3	5-5= 0	3-2= 1

SUBTRACTION FACTS: SUBTRACTING FROM 0 TO 5

Complete the following.
Use the number line to help.

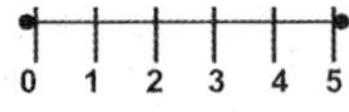

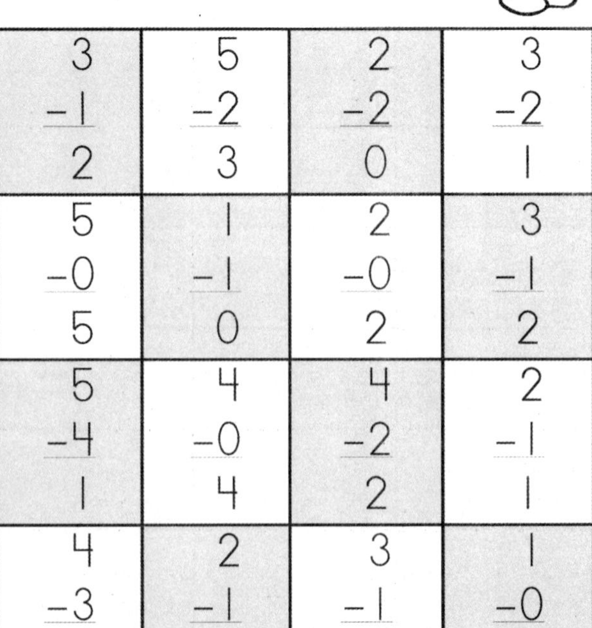

3 -1 2	5 -2 3	2 -2 0	3 -2 1
5 -0 5	1 -1 0	2 -0 2	3 -1 2
5 -4 1	4 -0 4	4 -2 2	2 -1 1
4 -3 1	2 -1 1	3 -1 2	1 -0 1

SUBTRACTION FACTS: SUBTRACTING FROM 0 TO 7

Complete the following.
Use the number line to help.

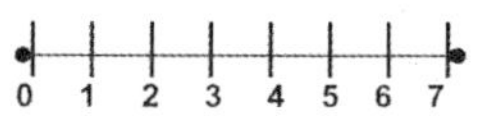

5-2= 3	1-1= 0	6-4= 2
7-4= 3	6-2= 4	7-3 = 4
3-2= 1	4-3= 1	6-3= 3
2-1= 1	7-5= 2	2-0= 0
7-1= 6	4-2= 2	5-3= 2
6-5= 1	6-1= 5	7-6= 1

SUBTRACTION FACTS: SUBTRACTING FROM 0 TO 7

Complete the following.
Use the number line to help.

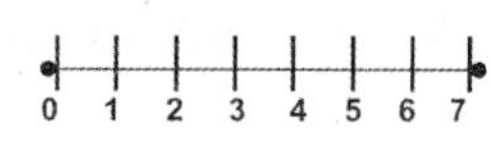

6 -3 9	3 -1 2	5 -1 4	7 -3 4
6 -2 4	3 -3 0	7 -4 3	3 -2 1
7 -5 2	4 -2 2	5 -3 2	6 -5 1
6 -1 5	4 -2 2	6 -2 4	7 -2 5

SUBTRACTION FACTS: SUBTRACTING FROM 1 TO 10

Complete the following sums
Use the number line to help.

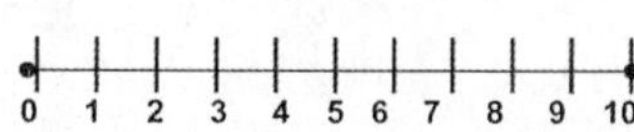

10-6= 4	9-6= 3	1-0= 1
4-2= 2	6-1= 5	8-3 = 5
10-7= 3	4-3= 1	6-3= 3
10-8= 2	9-5= 4	3-1= 2
10-5= 5	5-4= 1	8-4= 4
7-4= 3	6-1= 5	10-3= 7

SUBTRACTION FACTS: SUBTRACTING FROM 1 TO 10

Complete the following sums
Use the number line to help.

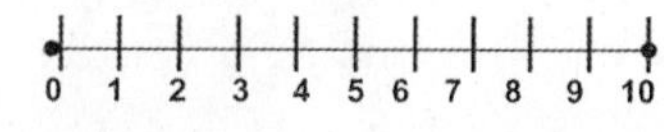

9 -2 7	1 -0 1	5 -2 7	10 -4 6
4 -3 1	5 -3 2	7 -6 1	8 -6 2
10 -7 3	10 -2 8	9 -1 8	9 -5 4
6 -2 4	8 -1 7	7 -5 2	3 -2 1

CERTIFICATE OF COMPLETION

Congratulations!

____

You completed this book!

Fantastic Work!